# EASTER

# EASTER

## A SPRING CELEBRATION OF TRADITIONAL CRAFTS AND RECIPES

TESSA EVELEGH

▼

PHOTOGRAPHY BY DEBBIE PATTERSON

▼

RECIPES BY JANE SUTHERING

▼

**Simon & Schuster**
New York  London  Toronto  Sydney  Tokyo  Singapore

For Richard, Zoë, Faye and Dragana

SIMON & SCHUSTER

Rockefeller Center

1230 Avenue of the Americas

New York, New York 10020

Copyright © 1994 Conran Octopus Limited

Text copyright © 1994 Tessa Evelegh

Photography copyright © 1994 Debbie Patterson

Recipe copyright © 1994 Jane Suthering

Designed by Prue Bucknall

Typesetting by op den Brouw Design and Illustration Consultancy, Reading, England

Printed in Hong Kong


10 9 8 7 6 5 4 3 2 1

Library of Congress Cataloging-in-Publication Data


Evelegh, Tessa.

  Easter: a spring celebration of traditional crafts and recipes /

by Tessa Evelegh.

    p. cm.

  Includes index.

  ISBN 0-671-88455-7

  1. Easter decorations. 2. Handicraft. 3. Easter cookery.

  I. Title.

TT900. E2E93 1994

745.594'1--dc20                                        93-28521

                                                        CIP

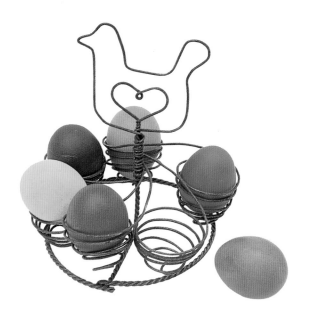

# CONTENTS

# INTRODUCTION

Nature is at her most exuberant in springtime. Lush foliage, in the freshest lettuce greens, and copious, brightly colored blooms push through seemingly barren earth in an astonishing show of color. This abundant display, all the more glorious following the cold, bleak months of winter, has prompted civilizations down the ages to welcome the season with a festival.

Our own celebration, Easter, is so entwined in the mists of antiquity, that even its name comes from an ancient pagan festival, celebrated in honor of Eastre, the Anglo-Saxon goddess of spring and fertility. To a large extent, many of today's customs have been absorbed directly from pagan rites. The gift-bearing Easter bunny, for example, is the modern representation of the Easter hare, which was considered to be an incarnation of Eastre. And the egg, now symbolic to Christians of Christ rising from the dead, is an ancient and universal representation of creation and rebirth.

Easter is the most important festival in the Christian religious calendar, commemorating the death and resurrection of Christ. A moveable feast, its timing is worked out each year according to the first full moon after March 21 which means it can fall any time between March 22 and April 25; the Eastern Orthodox Church has a slightly different calendar in which the holiday can fall a little later.

It is no accident that Easter coincides with the Jewish Passover, for it was during this feast that Jesus shared his last supper with his disciples. This link is echoed in the names given to Easter by many countries (France, *Pâques*; Italy, *Pasqua*), which derive from *Pesach*, the Hebrew for Passover.

In Christian countries, many customs and traditions centered around eggs have developed over the centuries. In addition to dyeing, decorating, and eating them, villagers throughout Europe would gather on the green for egg tossing and rolling, commemorating the rolling away of the stone from Christ's tomb. This custom was revived over 150 years ago by President James Madison's wife, who instigated Easter Monday egg rolling on the lawns of Capitol Hill, followed by an Easter Egg Hunt, events which are still celebrated today.

Lambs are another Easter icon, symbolizing the Paschal Lamb, which was the sacrifice offered at the Passover feast. Later, Christians came to see Jesus himself as the Paschal Lamb, offered as the ultimate sacrifice. Following the Lenten fast, Easter is a time of great feasting when tender new vegetables are served with celebratory roasted meats. Different countries have developed their own traditional egg dishes, breads, and cakes which are specially prepared for the Easter festivities. Chocolate Easter eggs, rabbits, and chicks did not appear until the middle of the last century and, since then, they have become the most popular Easter gifts, exchanged by all generations.

Traditionally, there is a widespread belief that the sun dances for joy on Easter morning, and people used to set off to the hills at sunrise to see the dawn. Certainly, Easter morning, whenever it falls, is the mark that spring has truly arrived. It offers the opportunity to celebrate this, the freshest and most colorful of seasons. The sheer abundance of blossoms, blooms, and greenery means there is plenty for picking with which to deck the home or offer as gifts.

This book is a celebration of spring, drawing inspiration from time-honored Easter customs to bring together a joyful collection of things to make, eat, and give. Together, they offer all the ingredients for a perfect Easter weekend, yet most can be treasured and enjoyed throughout spring and summer, as well as for years to come.

# EASTER
## TREATS

At Easter, nobody can resist the deliciously smooth and sensuously rich delights of chocolate. Molded into eggs, bunnies, and chicks, it is the traditional gift, exchanged by all generations. From decorated shortbread to marzipan animals, homemade candy is always the most appreciated.

# CHOCOLATE

Chocolate is a difficult and complicated ingredient to work with at home, and the only way that it becomes easier to handle is with practice. Professional chocolatiers spend years learning the intricacies of chocolate, so do not expect to make something perfectly the first time you try. If you are not happy with your results, do not throw out the chocolate. Gently melt it and use in any recipe calling for melted chocolate, such as candy, cake, or syrup.

Chocolate is made from several ingredients, and the most important when you are melting and using chocolate are the cocoa butter – a complex mixture of fats, each having a different melting point – and the sugar. If they are not melted correctly, the finished chocolate will not be beautifully shiny.

### MELTING CHOCOLATE

Chocolate should never come into contact with water or steam when it is melted, as either will cause the chocolate to thicken and lose its shine. There are various methods for melting chocolate, but the easiest one is to melt the chocolate in the oven on its lowest setting. Preheat the oven, then break the chocolate in

*LEFT* HANDMADE CHOCOLATE EGGS MAKE THE MOST SPECIAL EASTER GIFTS OF ALL.

equal-sized pieces into a clean, dry, ovenproof bowl and place it in the oven. The chocolate will melt slowly with no danger of cooking or burning. Stir the chocolate occasionally until it is smooth.

Chocolate can also be melted over simmering water. Cut or break the chocolate in equal-sized pieces, and put it in a clean, dry, double boiler over simmering water. Stir until the chocolate is smooth. It is a good idea to wrap a piece of foil around the top of the pan and set the bowl on the foil. This stops any steam from escaping at the side of the pan.

### TEMPERING CHOCOLATE

Before you can mold chocolate, it must first be warmed and cooled and then warmed again so the fats melt correctly. This technique is known as tempering. Unless chocolate is tempered correctly, it will not set quickly, making it difficult to remove chocolate shapes from their molds. A sugar thermometer is useful, but you can learn to temper chocolate from its appearance. When correctly tempered, it will be liquified but still slightly thick in consistency, and a small blob dropped on a cold surface, such as marble, should set within one minute. Tempered chocolate must be used immediately. If it is left to set or melted again, it must be retempered before it can be used for molding.

To temper chocolate, melt it until smooth, then place the pan of choc-

11

olate in a larger one containing cold water and a few ice cubes. Stir the chocolate continuously until some of it sets on the sides and bottom of the bowl. This will happen when the mixture is about 82°.

Warm the bowl of chocolate again until it is just melted and smooth. The temperature of the chocolate at this stage should be cool, about 84° for milk chocolate, 86-88° for dark chocolate and 84° for white chocolate.

### MOLDING CHOCOLATE
The temperature at which chocolate is molded is crucial. If it is too hot, a fat bloom (irregular streaks) will appear on the surface as it cools. If it is too cold, a sugar bloom will appear. Blooms on chocolate only detract from the appearance, however, and are not harmful to eat.

### HOLLOW EGGS
Molds are now usually made from Plexiglas, which makes them much easier to deal with than old-fashioned metal molds. Whichever type you use, however, the same rules apply. Make sure the mold is completely clean and dry. Polish the inside of the mold with a clean cotton cloth to make the surface shiny.

There are two ways of actually applying the chocolate. The first method requires a lot of melted chocolate. Using a large pastry brush, coat the inside of each half of the mold with tempered chocolate and leave it in a cool place to set, which can take up to 30 minutes. Then make a second layer by filling each half of the mold completely with melted chocolate, tapping the mold on the surface to remove any air bubbles. Pour out the excess chocolate, leaving the mold evenly coated. Leave to cool until the chocolate is "waxy" in consistency, then trim the edges with a small sharp knife to leave a smooth rim.

The alternative method requires far less chocolate. Pour enough tempered chocolate into each half of the mold to come about one-third of the way up the sides, then carefully swirl the chocolate around to coat the mold in an even layer. For both methods, leave the chocolate to set until it is completely brittle. It is better to leave the molds to set in a cool place, not in the refrigerator where condensation can affect the chocolate.

To remove the molds, gently tap them on a hard surface and the chocolate should pop out. If the chocolate does not loosen, gently tap the mold a few more times. If you still have difficulty, place the mold in the freezer for about 5 minutes. Resist the temptation to loosen the chocolate with the tip of a knife, as you could easily damage the edge.

Once the molds have been removed, join the two chocolate halves together. Warm the edges very slightly by placing the chocolate shapes on a warmed cookie sheet for a second or two, or by running a hot knife edge over the surface. (Heat the knife over a flame and not in hot water.) As soon as both surfaces are slightly melted, press them together and hold them for a few moments until they are set in position. Balance the egg in a small bowl and leave until completely set, which can take up to 30 minutes.

### SMALL SOLID EGGS
Polish the mold halves with a clean cotton cloth, then fill them with tempered chocolate. Leave to harden, then press the shapes out of the molds with your fingers. To join two halves, place them on a warm cookie sheet flat side down for a second or two until level, then press together. Leave in a cool, dry place to set completely.

Harlequin eggs can be made by sticking different-colored halves together, such as dark chocolate and white chocolate.

### CHOCOLATE RUNOUTS
Choose a template, such as an egg shape, rabbit, or chick (see pages 122-3) and draw the outline in pencil on a sheet of baking parchment. Stick the baking parchment down with a few dots of melted chocolate, then, using a paper pastry bag fitted with a fine writing tip, follow the outline of your shape. Leave to set.

Spoon melted chocolate into the center and, using a small skewer or toothpick, work it toward the edges to fill the shape completely. Tap the tray on the work surface to remove air bubbles, then leave in a cool, dry place to set.

The Easter eggs for the Chocolate Gateau on pages 116-17 are about 2 in. high and are made with white chocolate, piped with a tiny bow of melted milk chocolate.

### PIPING WITH CHOCOLATE

Adding a few drops of sugar syrup to melted and cooled chocolate will make it easier to pipe. The amount you add will depend on the type of chocolate, but as a rough guide use 15 drops to every 4 oz. milk or dark chocolate and about 25 drops to 4 oz. white chocolate.

Use the sugar syrup made for the Chocolate Gateau on pages 116-17, but omit the liqueur. Adding the syrup is a matter of practice, so always add it drop by drop and stir well. If the chocolate hardens, warm it gently again and let it cool to a piping consistency.

## CHOCOLATE PASTE RIBBONS

Add light corn syrup to melted chocolate and leave to cool, to produce a malleable paste which can be rolled out, cut into ribbons and shaped into decorative bows. The paste will set hard and brittle.

*4 oz. dark chocolate, broken into equal-sized pieces*
*4 tbs. light corn syrup*
*or*
*4 oz. white chocolate, broken into equal-sized pieces*
*2 tbs. light corn syrup*
*confectioner's sugar for rolling*

Place the chocolate with the syrup in the top of a double boiler. Warm gently over simmering water, stirring until just melted. Remove from the heat, stir and let cool. Alternatively, you can heat the mixture in a microwave on a medium-high setting until just melted, checking and stirring at 30-second intervals. Turn out on a marble slab and knead until smooth and cool.

ABOVE MOLDED EASTER EGGS DECORATED WITH CHOCOLATE PASTE RIBBONS AND PIPED WITH MELTED CHOCOLATE.

Either use immediately or cover with plastic wrap and place in a bag or store in a plastic container in a cool place.

To use, knead the paste until it becomes malleable once more – the heat of your hand should be sufficient. If not, warm the paste in a microwave on low setting (10%) for a few seconds. Roll out on a marble slab lightly sprinkled with confectioner's sugar, if necessary, to prevent the paste from sticking. Cut out ribbons, shape bows, and attach to the chocolate eggs by pressing, and leave to set firm.

# MARZIPAN ANIMALS

Marzipan was a traditional Easter sweetmeat long before chocolate grew in popularity. These marzipan Easter animals are decorated with Royal Icing (see page 17) and with edible food coloring. For the eyes you will need tiny dots of piped melted chocolate which have been allowed to harden. Before beginning, read through the instructions and assemble the necessary equipment. For decorating the animals you will need paper pastry bags fitted with fine writing tips, a small knife, and a fine paintbrush.

The shapes can take at least 24 hours to firm and harden. This is important because they can become moldy if they are not dried out completely. Store the shapes in airtight containers. Animals or eggs made with Marzipan will keep for two to three weeks.

*ABOVE* IRRESISTIBLE MARZIPAN RABBITS AND CHICKS ACCOMPANIED BY VIBRANT LADYBUGS AND PASTEL EGGS ROLLED IN COLORED SUGAR. THE SHAPED COOKIES ARE MADE FROM THE LEMON SHORTBREAD ON PAGE 17 AND FROM TRADITIONAL GINGER-BREAD (RECIPE NOT INCLUDED).

## MARZIPAN

This marzipan is made without raw egg. If you do not have a sugar thermometer, the sugar syrup is at the soft ball stage when it forms a small, soft ball if it is dropped into a bowl of very cold water.

*Makes a generous pound*

*1 cup superfine sugar*
*pinch of cream of tartar*
*8 oz. ground almonds*
*½ tsp. lemon juice*
*1 tsp. orange flower water, or a few drops natural almond essence*

Put the sugar, cream of tartar, and ½ cup water in a small saucepan over low heat and stir until the sugar and cream of tartar are dissolved. Bring to boil and boil until the temperature on a sugar thermometer reads 240° or is at the soft ball stage.

Immediately remove the syrup from the heat and stir in the ground almonds, lemon juice, and orange flower water, if using, with a wooden spoon. Mix to a firm paste. Flavor with a few drops of almond essence at this stage, if using instead of the flower water.

As soon as the mixture is cool enough to handle, transfer it to a marble slab or plastic board and knead until smooth and cool. Cover with plastic wrap and keep in the refrigerator. This paste will keep for two to three weeks. Seal completely to ensure it remains malleable.

## RABBIT

To make a rabbit, you need a scant ¼ cup uncolored marzipan and two tiny balls of pink-colored marzipan – one slightly larger than the other. These make the nose and tail .

Divide the uncolored marzipan into two pieces – one twice the size of the other. Shape each piece into an elongated pear-shape, then make a cut in the pointed end of each piece. The larger piece will be the body.

Position the larger piece of marzipan with the cut facing toward you. Twist each cut piece outward in a quarter-turn to make the legs.

The smaller piece of marzipan is used for the head. Holding it in your hand, with the cut at the top, twist the two cut pieces backward in a quarter-turn to make the ears.

Press the head onto the body, then stick on the nose and tail, with a tiny blob of royal icing.

Using a paper pastry bag fitted with a fine writing tip, pipe two eyes with royal icing, then top each with a tiny chocolate dot.

Using a fine paintbrush dipped in black edible coloring, make three dots on each side of the nose and three lines on each foot. Leave the rabbit in a cool, dry place to harden.

## CHICK

To make a chick, you need ¼ cup yellow-colored marzipan and a tiny amount of orange-colored marzipan for the beak.

For the top of the chick's head, roll out a tiny amount of yellow marzipan, then twist it into a coil.

Divide the remaining yellow marzipan to give a generous third and a scant two-thirds. Shape both pieces into balls – the small one is for the head. Shape the larger ball so it has a pointed end, which will represent the tail feathers. Make a cut on each side of the body to form the wings; then score a few lines along each wing for feathers with a small knife. Score markings around the tail as well.

Set the head on the body, then set the coil of marzipan on the head. Make two indentations on each side of the head with the handle of a small spoon to form the eye sockets. Using a paper pastry bag fitted with a fine writing tip, pipe two eyes with royal icing, then top each with a tiny chocolate drop. Shape the orange marzipan into a beak and press it into position. Leave the chick in a cool, dry place to harden.

*BELOW THE RABBIT AND CHICK ARE CONSTRUCTED FROM SIMPLE SHAPES.*

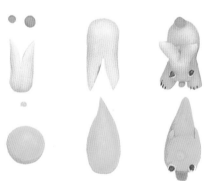

# EASTER BASKET COOKIES

*Makes 12-14*

LEMON SHORTBREAD
*1⅔ cup all-purpose flour*
*¼ cup rice flour*
*½ cup butter, softened, plus extra for greasing cookie sheets*
*¼ cup confectioner's sugar, sifted*
*finely grated rind of ½ lemon*

MALLOW PASTE
*2 tsp. powdered gelatin*
*2 tsp. shortening*
*3 cups confectioner's sugar, plus extra for rolling*
*green and yellow food coloring*

TO ASSEMBLE THE BASKETS
*1 egg white, lightly beaten*
*about 4 tbs. Royal Icing*

Lightly grease two cookie sheets with butter and preheat the oven to 325°.

Sift the flour and rice flour together, then rub in the butter until the mixture resembles fine crumbs. Stir in the sugar and lemon rind and knead to form a firm, pliable dough.

Roll out the dough on a lightly floured surface until about ⅛ in. thick and cut out basket shapes using the template on page 124. With a small knife, mark weave lines on the basket shapes. Place on the cookie sheets and bake for about 15 minutes until lightly golden. Cool on a wire rack.

To decorate, make six primroses and four leaves for each basket using mallow paste colored with food coloring. Once hard, attach these to the basket with royal icing.

To make the mallow paste, place the gelatin, shortening, and 3 tbs. water in the top of a double boiler over simmering water and heat gently until dissolved, stirring.

Sift the sugar into a bowl, then stir in the warm liquid. Place on a surface lightly dusted with powdered sugar and knead until smooth and cold. Cover with plastic wrap and then a tightly sealed plastic bag and store in the refrigerator.

To shape the primroses, use pale yellow paste. Roll out the paste thinly on a surface lightly sprinkled with powdered sugar. Cut out five tiny heart shapes for each flower (a petits-four cutter is useful for this). Press the five points together, sticking them with egg white. Leave on a sheet of baking parchment or rice paper until set and hardened, up to 24 hours. Paint fine lines in the center of each flower with yellow food coloring.

To shape the leaves, use green paste. Roll out the paste thinly. Cut out appropriate leaf shapes with small cutters or use a template. Mark veins on the leaves with a small sharp knife, then leave to set and harden.

## ROYAL ICING
*Makes about ½ pound*

*1 egg white*
*2 cups confectioner's sugar, sifted*
*1 tsp. lemon juice*

Lightly beat the egg white in a bowl. Beat in the confectioner's sugar, 1 spoonful at a time. When half the sugar has been added, beat in the lemon juice, then continue adding the sugar until a firm texture is reached. The icing can be stored in the refrigerator for up to a week.

*LEFT AND ABOVE* LEMON SHORTBREAD BASKETS MAKE DELICIOUS EASTER GIFTS.

# DECORATED
# EGGS

Symbolic of new life and fertility
since pagan times, eggs have come
to represent the resurrection. For
centuries, eggs have been embel-
lished and exchanged at Easter
resulting in a rich inheritance of
traditional crafts. Ranging from
simply dyed shells to intricate
works of art, decorated eggs can
add color to the Easter egg hunt or
become precious gifts to treasure.

# DYED EGGS

Colored eggs instantly evoke the image of Easter. Adding them to floral decorations transforms a simple spring arrangement into something festive. Placing them on the breakfast table revives that childhood thrill of anticipating a special day.

Yet, for all the magic they bring, eggs are easy to color. Being naturally porous, they take the pigment well, and the charm of dyeing them is that each egg holds an element of surprise. The imperfections of their shells and their individual "skin tones" affect the way the dye takes, resulting in marbled and speckled effects.

In the past, natural dyes were used, but nowadays there is a far wider palette to choose from: egg-dyeing kits and food colors for eggs that are to be eaten; or a rainbow of fabric dyes for those that are not. If the eggs are to be eaten, or likely to be subjected to a bit of rough and tumble in an Easter egg hunt, they should be hard boiled first. Put them into a pan of cold water and bring them slowly to a boil to avoid cracking, then simmer for a further ten minutes. Eggs to keep should be dyed raw in a cold solution and blown afterward; empty shells would float, and weighting them down could damage them.

To prepare the dye, mix the pigment – either half a bottle of food color or half a tablet of fabric dye – into about 2 cups of hot water. Add two tablespoons of vinegar and one of salt as fixative. The mixture should be a very deep shade – if it is not, add more pigment. Stir well and allow to cool. Lower the eggs in and leave until the shells have become the desired color. Drain them on paper towels and either leave natural or polish with a little cooking oil.

Once the eggs are completely dry, they can be blown. Very carefully, make a small hole at each end with a darning needle and, holding the egg over a bowl, blow out the contents. Rinse the shells in warm water and allow them to dry.

*LEFT* THE CHALKY GOLD OF TURMERIC AND THE BURNISHED COPPER OBTAINED FROM ONION SKINS SIT COMFORTABLY WITH BRIGHTER, MANMADE COLORS.

*LEFT* FERNS, PRIMROSES, AND EVEN THE LEAVES OF AN INDOOR GRAPE IVY MAKE EXCELLENT PRINTING PLATES.

*RIGHT* A LEAF OR FLOWER, AN OLD PAIR OF PANTYHOSE, AND DYE ARE ALL THAT IS NEEDED TO TURN EGGS INTO DELICATE WORKS OF ART.

# LEAF PRINTS

Through the ages artists have striven to imitate the beauty of nature, and there is no better way than to make a print directly from the original. With practice, even those who are unsure of their artistic abilities can produce exquisite designs using spring flowers and leaves as stencils when dyeing eggs. The prints can be made on undyed eggs to let the natural shell color show through. Alternatively, they can be applied to eggs that have already been dyed to a pale shade. This allows the flower or leaf motif to appear in a contrasting tone: the dye bleeds delicately around the edges and along leaf veins, sometimes appearing as slightly different hues.

The finer and flatter the original leaf or flower is, the better the end result will be, as these hug the egg closely, making a better mask.

Place the leaf or flower on the egg, flattest side down (this is usually the upper side). Lay a square cut from a pair of old pantyhose over the egg and tie tightly at the back. The leaves and petals will spread slightly as the fabric is tightened around the egg, so compensate for this in your arrangement. Lower this package into the dye and let the background color develop. When you are happy with the shade, remove the egg from the dye. Allow the egg to dry out completely before cutting away the fabric.

# NATURAL DYES

For centuries, the delicate, moody tones of natural dyes extracted from plants and minerals were the only option for coloring eggs. Some of these shades are still easily created using ingredients from the pantry; others require dyes that are more likely to be found in healthfood stores and pharmacies.

Highly effective, yet cheap and easy to work with, onion skins produce a range of hues from subtle yellow to burnished copper; red onion skins give more ruby tones. For a vivid, chalky yellow, try using turmeric (see page 20).

Less commonly found, but worth the effort for their subtle shades are redwood for red tones from dusky pink to deep crimson, and logwood for moody purples and denim blues. Although these are natural products, they are not suitable for dyeing eggs that will be eaten, nor should they be boiled in saucepans that are used for cooking any kind of food.

Whatever natural dye source you use, the pigment will have to be extracted by boiling in water. Use either six onion skins or two tablespoons of turmeric, redwood or logwood in about 6 or 7 cups of water. Add two tablespoons of vinegar to intensify the color, then simmer until a deep tone is achieved. Add more pigment material at this stage if necessary and continue

simmering until you are satisfied that the shade is deep enough.

If the eggs are going to be eaten, they can be boiled for ten minutes in the dye. If they are already cooked, leave them in the cooled solution for up to half an hour. The solution must be cold for eggs that are to be kept, as these will need to be blown afterward (see page 21), and any heat in the liquid will slightly cook and solidify the contents.

Remove the eggs with a wooden spoon to avoid damaging the delicate film of color, and drain on paper towels. When they are completely dry, either leave them with their natural, chalky finish, or polish them with a little cooking oil.

The joy of coloring with natural materials is that each dye behaves in a slightly different way. But as you acquire the dyer's skills and learn about the individual qualities of each dye, the palette broadens. Once you are confident with single-pigment dyes, you can mix the colors. For example, dyeing an egg pale yellow using turmeric, then dipping it in a blue solution of logwood can turn the shell a deep olive green.

# ENGRAVED EGGS

Engraved eggs are traditional in continental Europe, where many countries have developed their own distinctive styles. In the Ukraine, Lithuania, and Poland, the designs are often geometric, while Switzerland favors flora, fauna, and houses. However, they all share a charming simplicity. As eggs are engraved by scratching a design on dyed shells to reveal the natural shell color underneath, large areas of complicated engraving could weaken the shells.

Start with a simple design, such as a name and date, and progress to something more ambitious once you have gained confidence. An effective way to develop a design is to section the egg, either in concentric rings, or with a longitudinal line dividing it into "front" and "back".

Try to use an exacto knife in a scratching action rather than long, clean sweeps which could appear uneven. It is better to move forward only ¾ in. at a time, going back over the line, before moving on.

*LEFT* SIMPLE LINE IMAGES ARE EASY TO REPRODUCE WHILE GIVING THE EGGS AUTHENTIC APPEAL.

*RIGHT* TRADITIONALLY, EGGS WERE ENGRAVED WITH A SHORT EASTER MESSSAGE.

# BATIK EGGS

The brilliantly colored Pisanki eggs that are made in many East European countries are quite easy to reproduce at home with a little patience, practice, and care.

Using the batik wax-resist method of dyeing, the patterns are gradually built up, starting with the palest color and finishing with the darkest, which traditionally was almost black. Fabric dyes, which come in a broad palette of vibrant colors, are highly effective for this process (see page 21).

Work directly on the shell. A pencil design could smudge and be difficult to follow as successive dyes mask the lines. Even a series of concentric lines or zigzags running around the egg can be effective if done in rich, glowing colors.

### WORKING WITH WAX

Begin by dipping the egg halfway into a pale dye, such as yellow, to give a guideline around the middle. Once that has dried, the egg is ready for its first wax pattern.

Draw the design on the egg with hot wax using a tjanting needle – a special tool with a tiny metal funnel mounted on a wooden stick. Put a small piece of beeswax in the top of the funnel, and heat over a candle until the beeswax runs through the tiny hole in the other end. Tjanting tools, or batik needles from the Far East, old pen points and pins can all be used as drawing tools, each creating different effects, depending on their thickness.

Dip the egg in the first dye color. As the wax resists the dye, this first part of the design will show through as natural shell color on the finished egg once the wax has been melted off. When the egg is dry, draw on the second part of the design in wax and dip the egg in a darker dye. This will appear as the palest colored part of the finished design.

For more complicated designs, repeat the procedure using increasingly darker dyes; by the time the egg comes out of the final dye, it can look almost black. Carefully melt off the layers of wax over a candle rubbing gently with a cloth as the wax softens to remove any candle soot.

*RIGHT* INTRICATE DESIGNS CAN BE BUILT UP
IN LAYERS OF COLORED DYES.

1. HEAT THE FUNNEL OF THE TJANTING
NEEDLE UNTIL THE BEESWAX INSIDE IS FLUID
ENOUGH TO DRAW WITH.

2. DRAW THE FIRST PART OF THE DESIGN IN
WAX. THIS WILL SHOW AS NATURAL SHELL
ON THE FINISHED EGG.

3. DIP THE EGG IN RED DYE FOR A FEW
MINUTES TO COLOR IT PINK – A STRONGER
SHADE WOULD MASK SUCCESSIVE COLORS.

4. DRAW THE NEXT PART OF THE DESIGN IN
WAX, THEN PUT THE EGG IN A JAR OF
ORANGE DYE.

5. LEAVE THE EGG IN THE ORANGE DYE
UNTIL IT DEVELOPS A DEEP SHADE THAT WILL
CONTRAST WITH THE PINK.

6. DRAW ON THE FINAL PART OF THE DESIGN
AND DYE PURPLE. WHEN THE EGG IS DRY,
MELT OFF THE WAX AND GENTLY POLISH.

1. APPLY GLUE TO THE EGG AND WIND ON THE STRING IN SCROLL FORMATIONS.

2. COAT WITH AN OPAQUE PAINT, ALLOW TO DRY, THEN PAINT WITH TWO COATS OF GOLD SIZE.

3. WHEN THE GOLD SIZE IS ALMOST DRY, APPLY THE IMITATION GOLD LEAF. FINISH WITH A COAT OF SHELLAC.

4. BY GILDING ONLY OVER THE STRING, THE PAINTED UNDERCOAT WILL CREATE A PATTERN.

# GILDED EGGS

In 1290, the English king, Edward I, ordered eggs to be decorated with gold leaf for presentation to favored members of his court. Today, imitation gold leaf can be used to give stunning gilded results without the expense and difficulties of working with real gold leaf.

Prepare the eggs by blowing and washing them out (see page 21), then paint the shells with a water-based opaque paint such as Plaka. Once this is completely dry, paint with gold size – a special adhesive used with gold leaf. When the gold size is almost dry (see the individual manufacturer's instructions), carefully press the gold leaf onto the egg, and peel away its protective tissue. Allow the egg to dry for a day, then gently polish with absorbent cotton to rub away some

*ABOVE* THESE GOLDEN EGGS HAVE BEEN GIVEN A RICH UNDERCOAT OF COLOR FOR EXTRA DEPTH AND TO GIVE THE APPEARANCE OF ANTIQUE GILDING.

of the gold and reveal hints of color underneath. To prevent the gold leaf from tarnishing, finish with a final coat of shellac.

An alternative to smooth golden eggs, is to give them a texture before gilding. Even ordinary household string can be used to great effect.

33

# BEADED EGGS

From humble beginnings, the East European folk art of simply dyed Easter eggs became ever more elaborate and intricate. Eventually, they came to be used as love tokens, the depth of affection measured by the amount of painstaking work applied to so transient a canvas. The Polish custom of banging eggs together to see whose would break first did nothing to diminish the effort put into embellishing boiled eggs destined to be smashed and eaten.

Decorating Easter eggs first became popular on a wide scale in Europe during the thirteenth century. Red, symbolizing Christ's blood, was the traditional color. In Russia, the shells of these eggs were scattered on the graves of relatives on Easter Sunday. On the same day in Poland, dyed eggs were taken to church to be blessed by the priest, a custom still practiced by some.

In many countries, egg decoration became the preserve of single girls, who competed to create increasingly elaborate and intricate designs that could be presented as love tokens.

The ultimate egg love token was presented by Tsar Alexander III to his wife, the Tsarina Dagma, in 1884. It was the first egg to be commissioned from the royal goldsmith, Peter Carl Fabergé. Made of gold and white enamel, its golden "yolk" contained a miniature, ruby-eyed gold hen, which in turn opened up to reveal a tiny imperial crown set with diamonds.

Fabergé's style subsequently fired the imagination of generations of egg decorators to produce elaborately decorated eggs, some carefully hinged and satin-lined, and some, like the original, opening up to reveal a gift. A far cry from those real eggs that were decorated to last but a day, these jeweled versions are treasures to last a lifetime.

The beauty of eggs elaborately decorated at home lies in the individuality of each one. The romantic, richly beaded, braided, and brocaded eggs in Louis XVI style shown here have been evolved and perfected over the years by their maker. Wrapping fabric smoothly around an egg shape is very difficult to do, but you can create a similarly opulent effect using paint and even découpage as a background for beading.

Goose eggs may be more suitable than hens' for the more elaborate eggs – partly because they provide a much larger area for decoration and partly because they are considerably stronger. However, goose eggs do

*RIGHT* THE RICH, ALL-ROUND DECORATION OF THESE OPULENT EGGS IS EFFORTLESSLY SHOWN OFF BY HANGING THEM ON STRINGS OF GLASS BEADS IN FRONT OF A MIRROR.

1. PAINT A BLOWN GOOSE EGG WITH AN OPAQUE PAINT SUCH AS POSTER OR SATIN-FINISH HOUSEHOLD PAINT.

2. PASTE ON AN EASTER ARRANGEMENT, CUT FROM A GREETING CARD OR OLD PRINT. SEAL THE EGG WITH ARTISTS' VARNISH AND ALLOW IT TO DRY BEFORE APPLYING THE BEADED EDGING.

3. PLACE BROAD BANDS OF BEADS IN PERFECT ROWS BY LEAVING THE STRINGS IN PLACE UNTIL THE GLUE IS FULLY DRY.

sometimes come in extraordinary shapes, and need to be hand-picked at farms or gourmet stores.

One of the most basic difficulties egg decorators face is how to hold the egg while painting the whole surface evenly, without smudging or risking paint overlaps by painting in sections. One answer is to thread a fine skewer or knitting needle through the blow holes. This can then be laid on top of a bowl and the egg carefully rotated as it is painted.

The best adhesive to use for sticking any kind of decoration to an egg is a high-tack craft glue. It starts off opaque, so is easy to see while being applied, but dries clear. It also allows enough time before it sets for pieces to be moved around, yet is tacky enough to hold them in position while working.

For straight-line beading, buy beads that are sold on strings in craft and hobby stores, and glue them, still strung, into position. Wait until the adhesive is fully dry before removing the strings. Using this method, it is not difficult to cover an egg completely with tiny beads, the beads looking like stitches in fabric. Try using strings in alternating colors to create stripes, or even restring the beads to make elaborate patterns.

*FAR LEFT* RICH BEADING PROVIDES TAPESTRY-LIKE INSPIRATION. THIS EFFECT CAN BE ECHOED USING A DÉCOUPAGE IMAGE.

# E A S T E R
# GIFTS

Giving at Easter still reflects the spirit of yesteryear when the love, effort and obvious enjoyment of putting presents together mattered so much more than their commercial value. Handmade can mean something as simple as packing an Easter basket for the day, or creating something more long-lasting, like stitching a sampler to commemorate a special year.

# EASTER
# BASKETS

Many traditional Easter gifts – decorated eggs, flowers, chocolate, or other treats – hold few inherent surprises. But since these presents are so decorative in themselves, they deserve to be shown off rather than covered up. In short, Easter gifts should be not so much wrapped as gloriously presented.

Baskets overflowing with small presents for the whole family make a wonderful gift, evocative of abundant hampers from a bygone age. Buy a brand-new wicker basket as part of the present, or revive an old one by painting it in a springtime color. Spraying on the paint is the most successful method, as using a brush leaves paint clogged in the weave. Car spray paints are readily available and offer a wide choice of colors. To create an antique look with glimpses of the natural material showing through, simply spray the paint straight on the untreated basket. It will flake in areas where the surface is smoothest. This can be enhanced a little by gentle rubbing with a fine sandpaper. Line with paper or fabric before filling.

*LEFT* TRIM BASKETS WITH RIBBONS, BOWS, AND EVEN NESTS, THEN FILL TO BURSTING WITH EASTER GOODIES.

*LEFT* FOIL-WRAPPED AND SUGAR EGGS ARE
BEST SHOWN OFF IN GLASS JARS, STACKED
INTO A WIRE MILK CRATE.

The thrill of packed baskets is that they offer glimpses of their contents, while keeping secret the nature of items yet to be unpacked.

This idea can be extended to all kinds of easily portable containers which, if they are particularly relevant to the recipient, can become the present itself. Friends with green thumbs, for example, would be delighted with a seed tray packed with gardening delights (plus a chocolate egg or three). And who would not be enchanted by a prettily painted flat basket filled with hand-made Easter cookies?

Baskets and other containers lend themselves to witty displays of chocolate animals. The very best-quality chocolate creatures are wrapped in cellophane, rather than foil, to show off the full glossy detail of the chocolatier's craft. You can either pack these in a traditional basket as they are, or remove the cellophane and tuck them into alternative containers. Who could resist chocolate chickens roosting in old-fashioned terracotta pots? And what lady would not be delighted to open an exquisite hatbox to find chocolate baby bunnies snuggling in folds of tissue?

*LEFT* A BIRD CAGE BECOMES AN ELABORATE
BASKET FOR REALISTIC SUGAR EGGS.

SUBSTITUTED FOR A BASKET, A PACKED SEED
TRAY CAN LATER BE PUT TO GOOD USE
BY GARDENERS.

NOT AN EASTER BONNET IN THE HATBOX –
BUT CHOCOLATE BABY BUNNIES LAUGHING
AT THE JOKE.

STRING HANDLES TURN TERRACOTTA POTS
INTO RUSTIC BASKETS FIT FOR ROOSTING
CHOCOLATE CHICKENS.

EASTER BASKET COOKIES ARE TOO PRETTY TO
HIDE – A LONG FLAT BASKET MAKES A
PERFECT DISPLAY SURFACE.

# PASTA NESTS

Nests of colored pasta brimming with brightly dyed hard-boiled eggs make a charmingly simple Easter table decoration. Ribbons of fresh pasta are traditionally sold already twisted into portion-sized nests so all that needs to be added is a trio of eggs. Position the eggs while the fresh pasta is still soft; once it is dry, it will hold the eggs securely in place.

Delicatessens and gourmet stores offer standard buttermilk-colored egg noodles, as well as variously colored fresh pastas that are sometimes more difficult to find. Black pasta *(al nero di seppia)* is tinted with cuttlefish ink; the red *(alla bietola)* with beets, and the green *(verde)* with spinach.

If you cannot buy any of the colorful varieties, you can still achieve a festive look with the eggs. Food colorings offer a choice of safe-to-eat shades which can be used for a subtle or vivid effect, depending on how long you leave the eggs in the dyes. Here, the bronze eggs have been dyed using onion skins and the yellow ones using turmeric (see page 24). The soft green and the more extrovert, vivid turquoise color were achieved using food colorings.

*RIGHT* FRESH PASTA NESTS CONTAIN CLUTCHES OF DYED EGGS.

# PAPIER-MÂCHÉ GIFT BOXES

For generations, children in continental Europe have come down to breakfast on Easter morning to be greeted by an array of brightly decorated cardboard eggs, each containing a surprise gift. Following this custom, these charming, egg-shaped papier-mâché boxes are likely to become treasured themselves, long outliving their contents.

Decoration can be as simple as zigzags or spots if you are not a confident painter. For a more sophisticated effect, try using découpage. Paint the papier-mâché egg then stick down images using white glue. When the design is dry, apply a coat of diluted white glue to varnish and seal the egg.

### MOLDING THE GIFT BOXES

MATERIALS
*Round balloon(s)*
*Strips of cardboard*
*Newspaper*
*Wallpaper paste*
*Exacto knife*
*White latex paint*
*Poster paints*
*White glue*
*Polyurethane varnish*

Tear the newspaper into strips about 6 in. long by 1 in. wide and blow up the balloon until it is about 6 in. long.

Using plenty of paste, cover the balloon with one layer of overlapping paper strips placed top to bottom, then cover it again, this time placing the strips horizontally across the first ones. Repeat the whole process once more and allow to dry for a day. Over the next couple of days, repeat this process two more times, until you have built up 12 layers of newspaper strips. Allow the egg to dry out thoroughly.

When the papier mâché is hard and dry, draw a central line lengthwise around the egg. Using an exacto knife and following the line, cut right through the papier mâché and the balloon to divide the egg into two equal halves. Remove the scraps of burst balloon.

For the lip cut two strips of cardboard, one ⅜ in. wide, the other ¼ in. wide to fit snugly inside the cut edge of the egg. Glue the narrow strip inside the rim of one egg half, aligning the top edge of the cardboard with the top edge of the papier-mâché. Trim the strip to fit the egg if necessary. Allow to dry.

Glue the wider strip over the narrow one, aligning their bottom edges so that the top of the wider

*RIGHT* FANTASY BIRDS ADD TO THE APPEAL OF THESE BRIGHT-COLORED EGG-SHAPED GIFT BOXES.

1. PASTE 12 LAYERS OF PAPER STRIPS OVER A PARTIALLY BLOWN-UP BALLOON, ALTERNATING THE DIRECTION OF THE LAYERS.

strip projects above the egg's rim by ⅜ in. Allow to dry out completely. Trim the strip to fit.

Glue one layer of newspaper strips over the lip, then completely cover the egg with one more layer of strips, covering the hole left by the balloon's knot. Leave to dry out completely.

Paint the egg all over with white latex and allow to dry. Decorate the egg with Easter birds or patterns using bright poster paints and, when dry, finish with a coat of polyurethane varnish.

*LEFT* A FISTFUL OF JELLYBEANS BECOMES AN EXCITING SURPRISE WHEN HIDDEN INSIDE A PAPIER-MÂCHÉ EGG.

2. WHEN THE EGG HAS DRIED OUT
COMPLETELY, DRAW A CENTRAL LINE
AROUND THE EGG LENGTHWISE.

3. USING AN EXACTO KNIFE, CUT ALONG THE
LINE TO OPEN THE EGG, BURSTING THE
BALLOON AT THE SAME TIME.

4. FORM A LIP TO HOLD THE TWO HALVES
TOGETHER BY GLUING CARDBOARD STRIPS
TO THE RIM OF ONE HALF .

5. SECURE THE LIP WITH MORE PAPER
STRIPS. ALLOW TO DRY, THEN DECORATE
AND VARNISH.

# EGG AND FEATHER WREATH

In many cultures, the handsome, newly molted show feathers of courting male birds were often collected and woven into wreaths at Easter time. They were traditionally adorned with painted eggs, turning the circle into a symbol for rebirth. With a few easily obtainable materials, you can adapt this idea to make a welcoming Easter decoration for your front door.

Some craft and hobby stores sell small feathers by the bagful but offer the larger, more showy ones individually which means you can pick them out yourself. The superstitious will need to take care, however, as the elaborate feathers of some birds traditionally carry rather sinister connotations. Magpies, for example, were regarded as evil, while peacock feathers were believed to cause infertility if brought indoors. There is, nonetheless, a wide choice of feathers, including those from gamebirds and domesticated fowl. These range from the russet tones of pheasants' tail feathers to the brilliant shades of blue, green and gold provided by

*LEFT* THE TAIL FEATHERS OF MALE PHEAS-
ANTS FRAME A STRIKING WREATH.

exotic ducks and some bantam roosters.

A feather wreath, unlike many floral decorations, can be packed away to be used again year after year, perhaps given a new appearance with freshly decorated eggs.

CONSTRUCTING THE WREATH

MATERIALS
*Chicken wire, length of
wreath's circumference by
approximately 12 in.
Sphagnum moss
Approximately 20 large feathers
Bag of smaller feathers
10 decorated eggs
Glue gun and glue sticks
Florist wire*

First make the base. Tightly roll the wire around the moss to make a large sausage shape. Curve this into a circle and bind the ends together with florist wire. Then attach the feathers. Ideally, each feather should be wired separately to the wreath, though for speed, they can be attached using a glue gun. Start by arranging the large feathers in a pleasing formation. Fill in the spaces with plenty of smaller feathers radiating at angles from the base wire. Complete the wreath with decorated eggs. Either use painted wooden eggs or decorate your own fresh eggs and blow them before gluing in position with the heated glue gun.

5 1

# CROSS-STITCH ROOSTER

Cross-stitch samplers have a universal appeal that transcends time and place. There is nothing over-fussy about this form of embroidery which, since the 1830s, has been worked following charts similar to this one.

Traditionally stitched by young girls, they were often used to commemorate events such as births and marriages, incorporating lettering and dates. It is a delightful idea that can be reproduced today for any event. A small sampler takes only a short time to stitch and, complete with a personalized, embroidered message, it makes an original Easter card that can be kept and framed.

WORKING THE CROSS STITCH

MATERIALS
*32-count evenweave linen fabric,*
*12 in. square*
*1 skein each of stranded floss as shown*
*in key*
*1⅔ yd ribbon, to trim*

To center the motif: fold the linen in half lengthwise and work a line of

*LEFT* A PROUD ROOSTER, INSPIRED BY AN 18TH-CENTURY EMBROIDERY, LENDS A TIMELESS QUALITY TO THIS EASTER SAMPLER.

KEY One square represents two threads

| | | | |
|---|---|---|---|
| (yell) | DMC 782 | | |
| (sage) | Anchor 843 | (pink) | Anchor 10 |
| (dk gn) | DMC 924 | (red) | DMC 355 |

running stitches down the fold. Repeat widthwise. These lines cross at the center of the fabric and correspond with the thick rules on the chart. Work from the center outward. Using one strand of thread and counting two threads of linen for every square, follow the chart to stitch crosses in the correct colors.

To form a cross stitch, start by bringing an unknotted thread up from the back of the work, leaving a long tail, which can be secured later by passing the back of the cross stitches over it. Count two threads across and two threads up, pass the needle through to the back of the work, and bring it out to the front again exactly two threads below. Bring it across the original stitch to complete the cross. When working, make sure the top part of the stitch always goes in the same direction.

When the sampler is complete, measure out 4⅜ in. from both lines of central running stitches in both directions and pull out a thread. Cut along the line of removed thread. Remove the central basting markers. Place the sampler upside down on a thin white towel and gently press with a steam iron, spraying stubborn creases. Using tiny stab stitches, bind the sampler with ribbon, making loops at the corners.

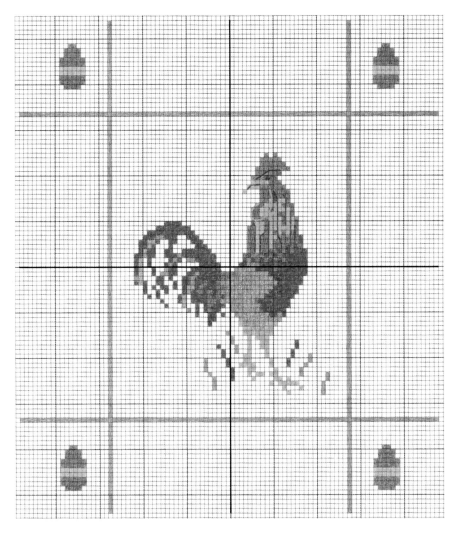

# PAPERCUT EASTER CARDS

Papercut collages in soft antique shades make original Easter greeting cards that can later be framed and hung on the wall. Inspired by a combination of traditional Swiss black-and-white papercuts and the more colorful Polish versions, they are built up layer on layer in different-colored papers to give depth to the scene.

In their simplest form, papercuts are made by cutting outline shapes from folded paper with scissors; they then open up into an image of perfect symmetry. Complex papercuts often incorporate intricate lace effects or images within frames that have to be cut using an exacto knife.

To make a collage papercut card, start by sketching the whole picture on a sheet of paper and cutting the backing card to size. When you have completed all the papercuts, arrange them on the backing card and glue them in position. They can be glued to the backing card using either spray adhesive or a paper-glue stick. The spray adhesive provides a fine film of

*LEFT* THE PERFECT SYMMETRY OF PAPERCUTS LENDS AN OLD WORLD CHARM TO HANDMADE EASTER GREETINGS.

glue which stays tacky long enough to allow the pieces to be moved around. The collage can be given more depth by attaching the pieces only where they naturally touch the backing card instead of gluing them down firmly around the edge.

Papercuts can be used for more than cards. The egg wraps shown here are very simple and bring an enchanting seasonal touch to the Easter morning breakfast table. Quick and easy to make, they can be cut mainly using scissors and need only minimal use of an exacto knife. They are a perfect introduction to papercutting and can even be used as

*LEFT* SOFT DENIM BLUES AND GOLDS ARE SYMPATHETIC COLORS FOR NATURAL EGGSHELL SHADES.

the ingredients for a collage card. Confident scissor users can then go on to more elaborate work with an exacto knife, such as intricate trellises and lace patterns. The choice of paper is important. Avoid paper that is too thick or very thin. Thick paper will be difficult to cut and thin paper may tear as you work.

CUTTING THE EGG WRAPS

MATERIALS
*1 sheet of construction paper
per 4 egg wraps
Tracing paper
Sharp embroidery scissors
Cutting board
Exacto knife
Masking tape
Invisible tape*

Trace the designs shown on this page. Fold the colored paper in half lengthwise. Starting at the top of the sheet, align the fold line on the pattern with the folded edge of the paper. Transfer the design. In the same way, mark a second design below the first, always positioning the fold line on the folded edge of the paper. There should be space for four egg wraps on the sheet of paper.

Use embroidery scissors to cut carefully around the outlines. Using masking tape, anchor the still-folded cutout on a cutting board. Cut around any internal lines, such as the area between the animals' legs, with an exacto knife. Unstick and unfold the paper creasing the fold line backwards. Attach the papercut around the egg using invisible tape.

FOLD
FOLD

# PAPIER-MÂCHÉ EGG CUPS

Instead of wrapping up Easter eggs, show them off on the breakfast table in handmade egg cups. This delightful fairytale example, beautifully decorated in delicate shades of turquoise and parchment, is made from papier mâché – newspaper strips and scraps of corrugated cardboard magically recycled into an exquisite but inexpensive miniature sculpture.

As they are small pieces, papier-mâché egg cups do not take long to make, so you can do several at once, though they will not be ready to decorate until the glue has dried completely. This takes about a day.

Papier-mâché egg cups are not washable, but if you give them a final coat of tough polyurethane varnish, you will be able to wipe them clean. Alternatively, tuck a small piece of linen into the egg cups to protect them from drips.

*ABOVE* THIS PAPIER-MÂCHÉ EGG CUP HAS BEEN FINELY DECORATED WITH GOUACHE PAINTS AND PEN LINES.

MATERIALS
*Sheet of corrugated cardboard,
8 in. x 7 in.
Sticky tape
Newspaper and white glue
China egg cup for mold
Vaseline
White latex
Gouache paints
Polyurethane varnish
Exacto knife and scissors*

1. USING AN EXACTO KNIFE AND THE TEMPLATE ON PAGE 124 AS A GUIDE, CUT TWO STAND SHAPES AND THREE RECTANGLES 2½ IN. BY 2 IN. FOR THE BASE.

2. ANCHOR THE STAND SHAPES ABOUT ¼ IN. APART ON ONE RECTANGLE BASE USING TAPE. STACK THE OTHER TWO RECTANGLES UNDER THIS AND TAPE IN POSITION TO GIVE DEPTH TO THE BASE. COMPLETELY COVER THE STAND AND BASE WITH SMALL NEWSPAPER STRIPS USING WHITE GLUE.

3. COAT THE INSIDE OF A CHINA EGG CUP WITH VASELINE, THEN PASTE FOUR LAYERS OF NEWSPAPER STRIPS TO THE INSIDE. WHEN COMPLETELY DRY, REMOVE THE PAPIER-MÂCHÉ SHELL FROM THE EGG CUP MOLD. TRIM THE EDGES INTO PETAL SHAPES USING SCISSORS.

4. GLUE THE EGG CUP TO THE STAND, THEN COVER THE WHOLE PIECE WITH ONE MORE LAYER OF PASTED PAPER STRIPS. WHEN DRY, PAINT WITH WHITE LATEX AND ALLOW TO DRY. DECORATE AND VARNISH.

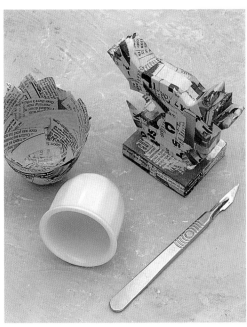

# SPRINGTIME SWEATER

Inspired by Native American art, this delightful jacket is designed with generous proportions for children aged three to ten and will not look out of place once Easter is over.

MATERIALS
*Rowan handknit D.K. cotton:*
*5(6:7:8) x 2 oz. balls, blue (A)*
*1(1:2:2) x 2 oz. balls each of*
*peacock (B), yellow (C)*
*1(1:1:1) x 2 oz. ball each of*
*mango (D), mustard (E), nut (F)*
*Pair each of No 6. and No 7. knitting*
*needles*
*Cable needle*
*Open-ended zipper, 12(14:14:16) in.*
*5 white buttons, ¼ in. diameter*
*5 black buttons, ½ in. diameter*
*Bright orange embroidery thread*

MEASUREMENTS
*To fit age 3–4(5–6:7–8:9–10)*
*Actual chest size: 34½(37:39:40½) in.*
*Length to shoulder: 15(16¼:17:18½) in.*
*Sleeve seam: 9½(11:12½:14¼) in.*

GAUGE
*19 sts and 28 rows to 4 in. over st-st on*
*No 7. needles*

RIGHT BUTTON EYES ADD TO THE APPEAL OF
THIS LIVELY SPRINGTIME SWEATER.

RIGHT A SINGLE BIRD FLIES
ACROSS THE SHOULDERS AT
THE BACK.

**beg:** begin(ning); **cont:** continue; **foll:** following; **in:** inches; **inc:** increase; **K:** knit; **P:** purl; **patt:** pattern; **rem:** remaining; **rep:** repeat; **rib:** ribbing: **RS:** right side; **st(s):** stitch(es); **st-st:** stockinette stitch; **tog:** together; **WS:** wrong side.

Figures in parentheses are for larger sizes. Repeat instructions in brackets [ ] as given.

## BACK

With No. 6 needles and B, cast on 78(86:90:94) sts. Work 2-color ribbing, stranding color not in use loosely across WS.

*1st rib row (RS):* K2B, [P2C, K2B] to end.

*2nd rib row:* P2B, [K2C, P2B] to end.

Rep 1st and 2nd rib rows 3(4:4:5) times more, inc one st at each end of last row for 1st size only. 80(86:90:94) sts.

Change to No. 7 needles.

Beg with a K row, cont in st-st.

Work 2(6:10:14) rows A and 2 rows D.

*Next row:* K2(0:0:0)B, 4(5:3:5)C, [4B, 4C] to last 10(9:7:9) sts, K4B, 4(5:3:5)C, 2(0:0:0)B.

*Next row:* P2(0:0:0)B, 4(5:3:5)C, [4B, 4C] to last 10(9:7:9) sts, P4B, 4(5:3:5)C, 2(0:0:0)B.

Work 2 rows D and 52(52:54:56) rows A.

Work bird motif from chart for back. Use separate small balls of A and E for each color area, twisting yarns tog

at every color change to link sts.

*1st row (RS):* K15(18:20:22)A, reading chart from right to left, K46 sts of row 1 of chart, K19 (22:24:26)A.

*2nd row:* P19(22:24:26)A, reading chart from left to right, P46 sts of row 2 of chart, P15(18:20:22)A.

Cont in this way until all 28 rows of chart have been completed.

Work 4(6:8:10) rows A.

Bind off loosely.

## LEFT FRONT

With No. 6 needles and B, cast on 38(42:42:46) sts.

Rib 8(10:10:12) rows as back, inc 2 sts evenly across last rib row on 3rd size only. 38(42:44:46) sts.

Change to No. 7 needles.

Beg with a K row, cont in st-st.

Work 2(6:10:14) rows A and 2 rows D.

*Next row:* K2(0:0:2)C, 4(2:4:4)B, [4C, 4B] to end.

*Next row:* P[4B, 4C] to last 6(2:4:6) sts, P4(2:4:4)B, 2(0:0:2)C.

Work 2 rows D and 2(2:6:10) rows A.

Cont in patt from chart for fronts, reading odd-numbered K rows from right to left and even-numbered P rows from left to right. Use separate small balls of yarn for each color area, twisting yarns tog at every color change to link sts.

Begin neck shaping on row 73 of chart, as indicated.

When all 82 rows of chart have been

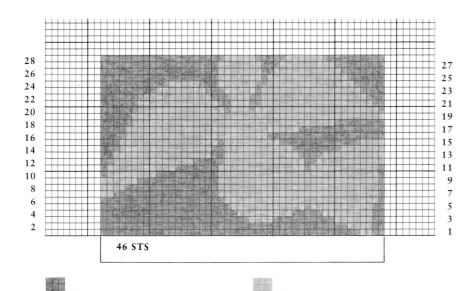

**46 STS**

A   E

*ABOVE CHART FOR BACK.*

completed, work 0(2:2:2) rows straight in A. Bind off rem 28 (32:34:36) sts.

### RIGHT FRONT

Work to match left front, reading each of the two-colored rows between D stripes from end to beg to reverse colors. When working from chart, read odd-numbered K rows from left to right and even-numbered P rows from right to left to reverse motifs and shaping.

### CABLE PANEL

Worked in A over center 8 sts of sleeves.
*1st row (RS):* P2, K4, P2.
*2nd row:* K2, P4, K2.

*3rd row:* P2, slip next 2 sts on to cable needle and hold at back, K2 then K2 sts from cable needle, P2.
*4th row:* As 2nd row.
*5th row:* As 1st row.
*6th row:* As 2nd row.
*7th row:* P2, slip next 2 sts on to cable needle and hold at front, K2 then K2 sts from cable needle, P2.
*8th row:* As 2nd row. These 8 rows form patt for cable panel.

### SLEEVES

With No. 6 needles and B, cast on 34(38:38:42) sts.
Rib 8(8:10:10) rows as back.
Change to No. 7 needles.
Cont in A.
*1st row(RS):* K13(15:15:17), work 8 sts of 1st row of cable panel, K13 (15:15:17).

*2nd row:* P13(15:15:17), work 8 sts of 2nd row of cable panel, P13 (15:15:17).
Work an additional 2(2:4:4) rows as set, working appropriate rows of cable panel at center.
***Next row:* K13(15:15:17)D, work 8 sts of cable panel in A, K13 (15:15:17)D.
*Next row:* P13(15:15:17)D, work 8 sts of cable panel in A, P13 (15:15:17)D**.
*Next row:* K0(1:1:3)C, 3(4:4:4)B, 4C, 4B, 2C, work 8 sts of cable panel in A, 2C, 4B, 4C, 3(4:4:4)B, 0(1:1:3)C.
*Next row:* P0(1:1:3)C, 3(4:4:4)B, 4C, 4B, 2C, work 8 sts of cable panel in A, 2C, 4B, 4C, 3(4:4:4)B, 0(1:1:3)C.
Rep from ** to ** once.
Keeping cable panel correct, cont in A, inc one st at each end of next and every foll 2nd(2nd:2nd:3rd) row until there are 64(56:48:72) sts, then on every foll 3rd(3rd:3rd:4th) row until there are 70(78:82:86) sts.
Cont straight until sleeve measures 9½(11:12½:14¼) in. from beg, ending with a WS row.
*Shoulder shaping:* Bind off 31 (35:37:39) sts at beg of next 2 rows.
Cont in cable patt on rem 8 sts until shoulder extension fits along bound off edge of front.
Bind off.

### FRONT BORDERS

With RS facing, No. 6 needles, and B, pick up and K 78(82:86:94) sts evenly along front edge.

Beg with a 2nd rib row, rib 5 rows as at beg of back.
With B, bind off evenly knitwise.

NECKBAND

Sew sides of shoulder extensions to bound-off edge of fronts and to 28(32:34:36) sts at each end of bound-off edge of back.
With RS facing, No. 6 needles and B, pick up and K90(94:94:94) sts evenly around neck.
Beg with a 2nd rib row, rib 7 rows as at beg of back.
With B, bind off evenly knitwise.

TO FINISH

Join bound-off sts of shoulder shaping to sides of back and fronts. Join side and sleeve seams. Sew in zipper. Using bright orange thread, embroider beaks and feet on birds in satin stitch and backstitch. With A, embroider a line of backstitch to divide rabbit's ears. For eyes, place one white button on top of one black button and stitch together on rabbit and birds.

*RIGHT* CHART FOR FRONT

F

E

A

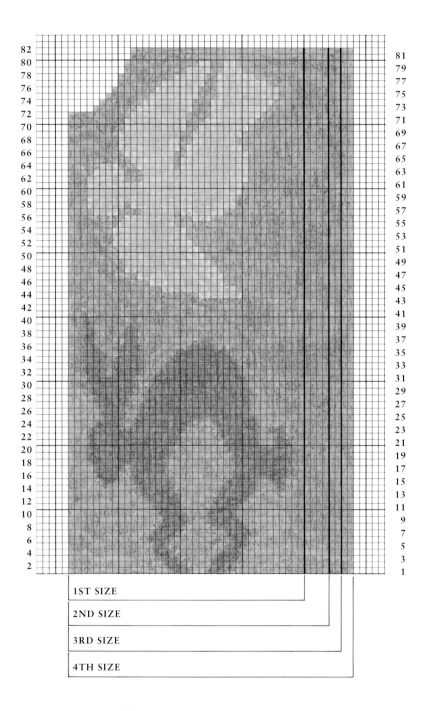

1ST SIZE

2ND SIZE

3RD SIZE

4TH SIZE

# EASTER APPLIQUÉ

Spring sunshine at Easter holds the promise of weeks of good weather. It is the time when thoughts turn from heavy winter coats to something alto-gether lighter, and a special family celebration at Easter offers the perfect opportunity to dress up in a new spring outfit that can last the whole summer through.

Appliqué is a charming way to give the simplest of children's garments an instant designer look. The running rabbits and spring flowers in this design are cheerful Easter motifs, perfect for the special day, but they will not make the clothes look out of place at other times, even in the height of summer. Either make a new outfit, such as this delightful gingham pinafore, incorpo-rating the motifs, or use the motifs to transform a ready-made garment. Alternately, stitch designs on a band of fabric and sew as a panel on a skirt, the side of a jacket, or even use it to lengthen a little girl's skirt. While this gingham pinafore has a wonderful old-fashioned charm, the rabbits and flowers would also look stunning on more casual clothes, such as a pair of bright-colored overalls, or even denim jeans.

Almost any fabric can be used for appliqué, but the motifs are much easier to handle if they are cut from a robust, tightly woven material, which is more likely to lie flat as you work.

## MAKING THE APPLIQUÉ

### MATERIALS
*Child's garment*
*Fabric remnants*
*Thin cardboard*
*Tracing paper*
*Sewing machine*
*Embroidery scissors*

First, make the template for the motif to be appliquéd. Using tracing paper and a soft pencil, trace the shape (see page 124). Cut it out and place on thin cardboard. Draw around this and cut out the cardboard shape. Check the shape against the original and adjust if necessary. Place the template on the right side of the fabric you wish to use for the motif and carefully draw around it with a soft lead pencil. Cut out the shape, allowing an extra ¼ in. all around. Place the fabric motif on the right side of the garment and baste it in position, across the middle, to make sure it lies flat. Following the pencil line, machine straight stitch all around the motif shape then, using very sharp scissors, carefully trim the motif as close as possible to the stitching. Set the machine to close zigzag stitch and restitch around the motif, covering both the line of straight stitching and the raw edge.

*ABOVE* SIMPLE MACHINE EMBROIDERY ADDS DETAIL TO THE APPLIQUÉD MOTIFS.

*RIGHT* RUNNING RABBITS AND SPRING FLOWERS LEND AN EASTER FRESHNESS TO A LITTLE GIRL'S DRESS.

An alternative method to using straight stitch for the initial anchoring is to use a fusable web, though this can be fiddly on small motifs. Lay the motif fabric on top of the fusable web and treat these layers as one. Using the template, draw the motif and cut out along the pencil line. Position the motif on the garment. Follow the manufacturer's directions to bond the motif to the garment. Finish the raw edge with zigzag stitch.

Decorate the appliqué with machine-embroidered stitches if you wish.

# EASTER
# BONNETS

Traditionally, it was considered good luck to put on something new on Easter Sunday, which is perhaps where the custom of wearing Easter bonnets originated. The Easter Parade was an opportunity to wear something more decorative after the inclement winter weather when hats had to be more practical. Easter, being the official mark of spring, meant brighter colors and prettier, more extrovert styles were *de rigeur*. And, after church, there was just a chance to turn a few heads during the promenade.

Now that formal hats are worn less, it is much more likely to be the children who are putting on Easter bonnets. They welcome any opportunity to don a hat, and brightly colored versions of Victorian styles are instantly appealing. Schools often organize Easter parades, giving parents the opportunity to re-live the Easter bonnet competition and help their children make ever more imaginative and extravagant hats.

*RIGHT* A JOYFUL COLLECTION OF BONNETS THAT CHILDREN WILL LOVE TO WEAR FOR THE EASTER PARADE CAN BE ADAPTED FROM ONE BASIC SHAPE WITH THE SAME DECORATIONS USED AGAIN AND AGAIN TO DIFFERENT EFFECT.

▼▼▼▼▼▼▼▼▼▼▼▼▼▼▼▼▼▼▼▼▼▼▼▼▼▼▼▼▼▼▼▼▼▼▼▼▼▼▼▼▼▼

## CONSTRUCTING THE HATS

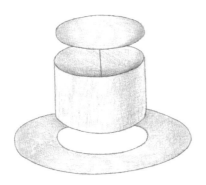

### BASIC HAT PATTERN

A hat consists of two main parts: the brim and the crown, which is made up of a side band and top piece. To make a hat, you first need to cut out a pattern. On paper, draw the rectangular side band pattern: the length is the child's head measurement plus 1 in.; the depth is variable according to the particular design. Cut out the side band and shape it into a tube, overlapping by 1 in. at the back. On a large piece of paper, draw one circle the diameter of the tube for the top piece and a larger circle around it to make the brim. (A simple way to draw large circles is to tie a pencil to one end of a piece of string the length of the radius, and anchor it with a thumbtack at the other end.) Cut out the circles.

When constructing the Easter hats, refer back to this basic pattern when component patterns are required.

## TOP HAT

MATERIALS
*Plain paper for pattern*
*2 large pieces of green poster paper*
*Large piece of embossed red paper*
*Large piece of embossed green paper*
*Large sheet of plain red paper*
*Large sheet of plain green paper*
*Paste and scissors*

Make a paper pattern for the side band to a depth of 8 in. Divide this into eight equal sections with pencil lines (a). Cut along these lines, leaving the bottom edge joined. Place on a new piece of paper, spreading the cut sections to create a $\frac{3}{4}$ in. gap between each at the top edge (b).

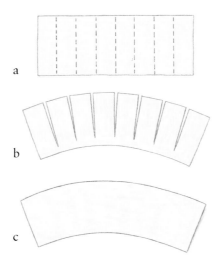

Draw around this shape and cut out (c). Bend the pattern into a tube and cut out a top circle. Cut a 2½ in.-wide brim to fit the narrower end.

Cut the hat from green poster paper, using the pattern, but adding ⅝ in. allowance at the top of the side

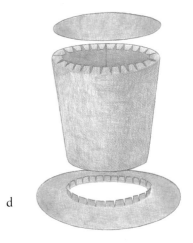

band and at the inner edge of the brim. Score the paper along the line of the original pattern and cut Vs into the allowance to make tabs.

Construct the hat, gluing the tabs as shown (d). Cover the brim and top with red embossed paper and the side band with green.

Trim the top and brim with half rosettes and attach folded spirals to the brim in long loops (page 125).

▼▼▼▼▼▼▼▼▼▼▼▼▼▼▼▼▼▼▼▼▼▼▼▼▼▼▼▼▼▼▼▼▼▼▼▼▼▼▼▼▼▼▼

## POKE BONNET

### MATERIALS
*Plain paper for pattern*
*Large piece of pink poster paper*
*Large sheet of pink paper*
*Large sheet of fuchsia paper*
*2⅓ yds. satin ribbon*
*Paste and scissors*

Make a paper pattern for the hatband. Divide the pattern into eight equal sections with pencil lines (a). Fold small darts along these lines to make the top edge shorter than the bottom (b). Place on a new piece of paper and cut out the new pattern. Trim the edge as shown (c). Cut a circle to fit the top diameter; and a 6 in.-wide brim to fit the lower diameter.

Divide the brim into eight with

a

b

c

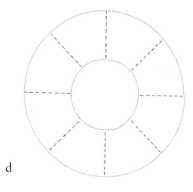

d

e

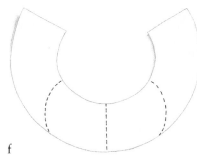

f

pencil lines (d). Pinch along these to make darts every 1 in. at the outer edge; tape the darts flat (e).

Cut through the pattern and then cut out the front section as shown (f). To calculate this, use ⅔ of child's head measurement. Measure out half this figure on the inside curve to the left of center and half to the right. Draw a curved line from these points to the front of the brim. Using the patterns, cut the side band and top

piece from pink poster paper (allow for tabs) and construct the crown. Cut a brim from each of the pink and fuchsia papers, adding an extra ⅝ in. to the shorter curve edge for tabs.

Fold the two brim pieces in half together across the middle, then make pleats outward from here. Trim the

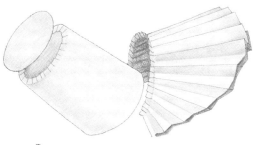

g

outer edge into points. Glue to the inside of the crown by the tabs.

Cut a rectangle of fuchsia paper 18 in. by the length of the radius and narrowly pleat it. Form it into a circle, stick the ends together and fix to the top piece. Make folded rosettes (page 125), attach around the base of the crown, add one to the top of the hat. Staple on satin ribbon ties.

# ORIGAMI CHICKS AND DUCKS

Broods of bright-colored paper chicks and ducklings perched along the windowpane make delightful, easy-to-construct Easter decorations. They are classic designs in origami, the Japanese craft of paper-folding, which is believed to be more than 1,000 years old. Even today, origami is a popular pastime in Japan, where it is used to make *noshis* (folded tokens) and elaborate gift packaging.

The secret behind the charm of these chicks and ducklings lies in the choice of paper. Sunshine yellow paper, some plain, some decorated with hounds-tooth check, adds a seasonal feel. The less complicated forms of origami, like the two pieces shown here, are not difficult to make, but newcomers to the craft might want to practice on plain paper until they are familiar with all the folds.

Almost any paper can be used as long as it creases into crisp folds without stretching or tearing. Paper sold especially for origami is often colored on one side and white on the other to add depth to the finished

*LEFT* OLDER CHILDREN CAN HELP WITH THE EASY-TO-FOLD ORIGAMI DUCKS AND CHICKS FOR AN ATTRACTIVE EASTER DISPLAY.

piece of work. In Japan, it is sometimes sold patterned on one side, solid on the other. The same effect can be achieved by gluing two pieces together back to back with spray adhesive or paste, and allowing them to dry completely before starting to make folds.

Both the chick and the duck are made from squares, and it is important to cut the paper to shape accurately. To make a square from a rectangular piece of paper, place the paper on a hard surface with the narrow edge nearest you. Fold up the bottom right corner so the bottom edge of the paper lies exactly on top of the left-hand edge. Make a firm crease along the diagonal. The top layer of paper now forms a triangle. Fold the underneath projecting paper along the edge of the triangle. Crease. Cut along the crease. For full folding instructions for the chick and duck, see pages 120-21.

Successful origami relies on accurate, firm folding and creasing. Work on a hard surface and, for crisp results, run the back of your thumbnail down each crease before going on to the next.

Sometimes, the paper is simply folded in place. At other times, it is precreased and opened up before the fold is made. It is important not to hurry these steps, as the precreasing means that when a more complicated fold is being made, every part falls neatly into the correct place.

# S P R I N G
# FLOWERS

Nothing can be a more dramatic manifestation of rebirth than the explosion of flowers around Easter time. Blooms burst from unpromising twigs, and flowers push through bare earth in an exuberant show of color that is never quite matched at any other time of the year. Celebrate nature's own New Year by gathering a small part of the bounty to enjoy indoors.

# CELEBRATION GARLAND

An important festival in its own right, Easter is a natural time to celebrate and is often chosen as a time for personal rejoicing. Weddings and christenings are especially popular at this time and warrant lavish floral decorations. Garlands are a universal hallmark of welcome and celebration; festoons of flowers say that a person or occasion merits the unsparing best of everything.

Usually made using cut flowers, garlands are normally expected to last only a day or two. To look fresh through the Easter holiday, however, requires a more lasting beauty. The garland shown here has been made with potted plants. This altogether more sensitive way of using flowers allows the garland to be dismantled once the blooms are over, and the individual plants can be planted in the garden ready to flower again next year. Pansies and primroses were chosen because they are hardy and easy to find, whether Easter is early or late.

Each season of the year has its own predominant colors, so the secret behind giving a garland a

*LEFT* A FESTOON OF SPRING FLOWERS, IN JOYFUL YELLOWS AND GOLDS, MARKS THE SEASON'S CELEBRATIONS.

*LEFT* PAINTED EGGS ADD EASTER'S
TOUCH TO A SPRING GARLAND.

## CONSTRUCTING THE GARLAND

### MATERIALS
*Small potted plants, about 6-10
per 12 in. of garland
Chicken wire the length of
garland and 2½ times
the width of shelf
60-80 florists' stub wires
(20 gauge)
Small terracotta pots, 2 per
12 in. of garland
Black plastic trash bags
Sphagnum moss*

springtime personality is to use shades of color which are traditionally associated with Easter.

Instead of dipping into the extensive palette of cultivated primrose colors, this garland is based on the simple shades of the woodland variety. Violas and pansies have been added, giving a whole range of subtle yellows from an almost papery off-white through to butter and deep golds, then softening to apricot and peach tones. With the addition of just one or two pansies in old rose shades, the garland takes on an enchanting Victorian feel.

To give the garland extra form, the primroses have been planted in old terracotta pots, their soft tones blurred further by the bloom of age complementing the peachy shades of the pansies.

Garlands must be in proportion to their surroundings: they will look meager if too small, but will be overpowering if too large. For pleasing proportions, cut the chicken wire base to two-and-a-half times the width of the shelf, mantelpiece, or lintel it is to rest on, and use plenty of plants for a lush look. Cover any exposed wire with moss.

Water plants and allow to drain. Pass a stub wire through the hole at the bottom of each pot, bend it in half bringing the ends together at the rim, then twist together and bend to form a hook. Plant a primrose in each pot.

For the remaining plants, cut the black plastic trash bags into squares large enough to hold a rootball. Take each plant from its pot and place it in the center of a square. Gather the plastic around the roots and loosely wind a stub wire around the neck to secure and enclose the rootball.

Roll and scrunch the chicken wire into a loose sausage shape and secure the bagged plants to this using stub wires bent in half in a hairpin shape. Attach a planted terracotta pot at intervals of about 6 in. Finally, fill in the gaps with moss.

1. USE SMALL PLANTS RATHER THAN CUT
FLOWERS FOR A GARLAND THAT WILL STAY
FRESH ALL EASTER.

2. RESERVING THE PRIMROSES, REPOT THE
PLANTS IN PLASTIC, THEN ATTACH THE
"BAGS" TO THE CHICKEN WIRE.

3. WIRE AND PLANT TINY
TERRACOTTA POTS WITH PRIMROSES TO
LEND A STRUCTURED GARDEN FEEL.

4. ADD MOSS TO CONCEAL THE CHICKEN
WIRE AND GIVE A WOODLAND QUALITY AND
DEPTH TO THE FINISHED GARLAND.

# SPRING'S BOUNTY

Nature seems to make a special effort in spring, putting on her most flamboyant apparel as if compensating for the long barren months of winter. The shades at this time of year are strong and clear: the vivid yellows of primroses, daffodils, cowslips, and some tulips; the brilliant blues of hyacinths, bluebells, and forget-me-nots; the deep magenta and pinks of hyacinths, cyclamen, and many tulips. When set against the fleshy emerald green of spring leaves, these colors are further intensified.

Spring also specializes in abundance. Flowers crowd the countryside as if gathering for a festival; they increase their numbers in the garden unaided, and they mass in the marketplace, all offering a plentiful supply of inexpensive blooms. Therein lies the secret of successful Easter displays. It is always better to buy armfuls of inexpensive flowers for a lavish show rather than to settle for a paltry one.

*LEFT* AN EASTER GATHERING OF FLOWERS –
AURICULA, TULIPS, TINY RED SEDUM,
CYCLAMEN, PINK AND BLUE HYACINTHS,
CHERRY BLOSSOM, LENTEN ROSE
(HELLEBORE), NARCISSI, VIOLA, LILY OF THE
VALLEY, COWSLIPS, PRIMROSES,
FORGET-ME-NOTS, AND WALLFLOWERS.

# EASTER POSIES

The charm of a posy is that it evokes the romance of the Victorian age. During that time, well-dressed young ladies carried posies, coquettishly using them in courtship. The restrictions imposed by the segregation of boys and girls and men and women led to the development of a whole language of flowers.

A gentleman would present his chosen lady with meaningful flowers; in reply, she would carry a relevant posy. It was a custom fraught with problems, however, as different dictionaries listed different meanings and, even when these were broadly in agreement, the courtship had to rely on the correct interpretation of subtle variations of meaning, often within one flower. A rose generally signified love, but to be presented with a yellow rose could mean jealousy, while, according to one dictionary, to receive the rose known as La France would be to receive an invitation to a moonlight meeting. To miss that message could perhaps divert the course of a young lady's future irredeemably.

Posies are most beautiful and authentic when composed of just one or two types of flower, mimicking the restrictions of the past that were imposed by the need to convey a clear, unambiguous message.

Alternately, choose a closely matched color scheme, such as woodland primroses with their enchanting cowslip cousins, or headily scented, pure white lilies of the valley with white forget-me-nots. Teaming different-colored varieties of the same flower can be delightful, too. Delicate

*LEFT* ARRANGED AS BOUQUETS, SPRING
FLOWERS CAN SIMPLY BE UNWRAPPED AND
PUT STRAIGHT IN CONTAINERS.

*RIGHT* TRADITIONALLY, POSIES WERE POEMS
PRESENTED WITH A SMALL BOUQUET OF
FLOWERS, BUT HERE THE PLAIN PAPER REPRE-
SENTS THE POEM AND THE FLOWERS CARRY
THE MESSAGE INSTEAD.

purple-and-yellow violas look wonderful massed with plain yellow ones.

More sophisticated combinations
could be achieved by combining the
magenta of tiny woodland cyclamen
and wild forget-me-nots in tones of
sapphire and amethyst, or by mixing
azure bluebells with orange, pink, or
red ranunculus.

MAKING A POSY

Before assembling the flowers, cut
about ⅜ in. off the end of each stem
using sharp shears, and put them in a
bucket of warm water for a long
drink.

The professional way to arrange
flowers into a posy is to cross the
stems, which gives each flower the
space it needs without being crushed,
while making the bunch look more
generous. This simple idea needs practice, however. One trick is to form
one hand into a "vase" by making a
circle with fingers and thumb, then
"arrange" the flowers in it. The posy
can then be wrapped – solid-colored
paper shows off the flowers best –
ready for giving.

## THE LANGUAGE OF SPRING FLOWERS

| | |
|---|---|
| **Anenome** – *Forgiveness* | **Narcissus** – *Egotism* |
| **Auricula** – *Painting* | **Pansy** – *Thoughts* |
| **Bluebell** – *Reliability* | **Pink** – *Pure love* |
| **Cowslip** – *Thoughtfulness* | **Primrose** – *Young one* |
| **Cyclamen** – *Timidity, shyness* | **Ranunculus** – *Radiant charm* |
| **Daffodil** – *Respect* | **Tulip** (red) – *I love you* |
| **Forget-me-not** – *True love* | **Tulip** (yellow) – *Hopeless love* |
| **Hyacinth** – *Playfulness* | **Tulip** (variegated) – *Beautiful eyes* |
| **Lily** – *Purity* | **Violet** – *Humility* |
| **Lily of the valley** – *Return of* | **Wallflower** – *Faithful against* |
| *happiness* | *the odds* |

# THE LOVELINESS OF LILIES

Breathtakingly beautiful and symbolic of purity, white lilies are traditionally used as altar decorations at Easter time.

With their sculptural form and sweet, heady perfume, radiant *longiflorum* lilies make an elegant focus for this beguiling outdoor scene. Although bought as cut flowers, these lilies have been arranged as if they are growing outdoors in a rich, mossy bed that is backed by a twiggy garden frame interwoven with trailing clematis. Terracotta pots of white scilla, delicate lily of the valley, and old-fashioned, dusty-toned auricula have been added along with a group of tiny bantams' eggs, a large goose egg, and a handmade nest containing quails' eggs. The finished arrangement evokes all that is delightful about a gentle, clear spring day – fragrance, delicate flowers and burgeoning new life, symbolized by the eggs.

The inherent elegance of lilies makes them easy to arrange. Just two stems placed in a tall vase create a beautiful still life without the need for added foliage.

The lily has always been regarded as a flower of unmatched loveliness. Worthy of kings and emperors, it appeared in paintings on the walls of Cretan palaces over three thousand years ago and inspired bronze capitals on columns in Solomon's palace. The New Testament exhorts us to "Consider the lilies. Even Solomon in all his glory was not arrayed like one of these".

Botanists believe that the lily revered in the past for its beauty was the Madonna lily, native to Palestine and sought for its rarity value, possibly because it is notoriously hard to grow. This same lily has appeared in Christian art through the centuries symbolizing purity and chastity. In pictures of the Annunciation, Gabriel is sometimes shown carrying a lily, and Joseph holds one in his hand to signify Mary's virginity.

For hundreds of years, the hard-to-please Madonna lily was the only one available to gardeners, but new varieties have now been discovered, often at great cost. When the young English botanist, Ernest Henry Wilson, discovered the exquisite regal lily (*Lilium regale*) on the borders of Tibet at the turn of the century, he was determined to send a good supply back to the Arnold Arboretum, his Boston employers. On one expedition, falling rock smashed his leg as he was crossing a narrow gorge, and he had to lie still as the rest of the party, including 50 mules, stepped over him. Thankfully, his leg was saved, and his prize was 7,000 bulbs to send home.

Until recently, Easter lilies were grown mainly in Holland and Belgium for export, and they used to be flown across the Atlantic specially for the springtime celebrations. They have become so popular that now they are grown on the northern Pacific coast, in Florida, Louisiana, and Texas for the occasion.

An alternative to cut flowers in an Easter arrangement is to use growing lilies which can then be either potted or transferred to the garden to bloom year after year, once the indoor display is over its best.

With the introduction of new hardy hybrids, lilies have shrugged off their old reputation for being difficult to grow. Many will flower every spring or summer with little help. Buying a variety that suits your soil (some hate lime) and making sure it is comfortably bedded down are the main priorities. While some species develop feeding roots at the bottom of the bulb, others have them above it and need to be planted at least three times the depth of the bulb. Planted in humus-rich soil in a sand-lined pocket to prevent rotting and slug attack, they should thrive with very little attention producing more flowers each year.

LEFT THE GREENISH-WHITE TRUMPETS OF THE LONGIFLORUM LILY MAKE A STUNNING FOCUS IN AN ELEGANT EASTER DISPLAY.

# BLOSSOM TREE

Clouds of blossom bursting from bare twigs are the epitome of spring – life emerging from the apparent death of the winter tree. It is a lovely idea to bring in some bare branches a few weeks before Easter, then watch the blooms burgeon and clamor for space on the laden boughs.

The blossom tree was one of Queen Alexandra of England's favorite Easter rituals, although it is not a particularly common custom in Britain. The Easter tree is much more likely to be seen in continental Europe or in America. In Germany, silver birch branches are traditionally brought indoors, the shimmering bark and tiny, unfurling lettuce-green leaves providing a delightful framework on which to hang painted wooden eggs.

The idea can be copied using many kinds of branch: sculptural larch, its bare limbs trimmed all winter long with miniature cones that are later joined by tiny bunches of vivid green needles and tufts of crimson blooms; varieties of pussy willow, ranging from those that bear neat, silky, silver cushions to those with fatter, more flamboyant flowers in shades of burnt rose; or branches cloaked in cascades of greeny-yellow catkins that sway in the wind.

For sheer abundance, nothing can match delicately scented fruit blossoms, which dance in the breeze like myriad ballerinas. These range from the purest white pear through pink-budded apple that pales as it opens, to the generous blush-pink of ornamental cherry and even stronger shades on some of the cultivated crab-apple trees.

Nurseries and florists are a good source of spring branches of all types. If you are cutting them from the yard, use sharp shears and cut at an angle away from and just above a new, outward-budding node. This way, there will be less damage to the branch, and it will be encouraged to thicken out over the summer.

It is easy to make a stunning display from any size of spring branches as there is so little arrangement involved. Very often, just three or four branches are enough to create a pleasing balance. Cut to size with sharp shears, they can be supported by a ball of chicken wire, scrunched to shape and fitted into a sturdy container. Chicken wire is a better choice for anchoring branches than florists' foam, which is soon broken up by the thick, woody stems. Wire also allows for slight movement, which creates a much more natural overall effect.

Terracotta urns and plant pots are a good choice of container for this kind of display as they offer a refreshing outdoor look, as if a corner of the backyard has been brought inside.

Easter trees need very simple decoration. Eggs of all types are an obvious but nonetheless pleasing option, their shape providing a smooth, uncluttered foil for the dense blossom. Hens' eggs can be dyed, painted, engraved, or gilded before being hung on the tree, or for a natural look, you can choose some of the less familiar domestic fowls' eggs – such as tiny speckled quail eggs, bantam eggs, duck eggs in shades of delicate blue green, or generously proportioned goose eggs. Prepare them by making a pin prick at each end, then blowing out the contents and thoroughly rinsing with warm water. To hang the eggs on the tree, make a loop at one end of a length of florist wire and thread a ribbon through this. Feed the other end through the egg. Trim the wire and turn up the protruding end to support the bottom of the egg.

Another idea is to deck out Easter trees with small gifts. These could be trios of tiny, foil-wrapped chocolate eggs, perhaps packaged in a twist of cellophane and tied with raffia; miniature filled baskets; or Easter cookies looped through with a length of ribbon.

*RIGHT* CLOUDS OF WHITE PEAR BLOSSOM HUNG WITH PALE BLUE DUCK EGGS ON DIAPHANOUS RIBBON CELEBRATE THE FRESHNESS OF SPRING.

## FASHIONING A FLORAL EGG

MATERIALS
*Terracotta pot*
*Black plastic trash bag*
*Block of florists' foam*
*Green florists' tape*
*Stub wires (22 gauge)*
*Approximately 24 miniature*
*spray roses*
*Bun moss*

Before starting, thoroughly soak the florists' foam and condition the flowers by cutting off the ends of the stems at an angle using shears. Soak them in tepid water for several hours or overnight. You can leave the terracotta pot as it is or paint it to complement the scheme.

Line the pot with a piece of black plastic, then cut the florists' foam into pieces and build up into an egg shape. Tape it into position in the pot and add a little moss around the rim of the pot.

Form "ribbons" of bun moss to divide the egg into quarters vertically and anchor it in place with stub wires bent to form a hairpin shape.

Using garden shears, trim the rose stems to about 2 in. then push them into the foam to make a compact arrangement completely covering the exposed foam.

1. A TERRACOTTA POT, FLORISTS' FOAM, BLACK PLASTIC, AND FLORAL TAPE PROVIDE THE FOUNDATIONS.

2. CAREFULLY BUILD UP THE FLORISTS' FOAM INTO AN EGG SHAPE, THEN TAPE IT IN POSITION.

3. QUARTER THE EGG WITH BUN MOSS, ANCHORING IT IN PLACE WITH BENT STUB WIRES.

4. THE TINIEST SPRAY ROSES MAKE THE MOST SUCCESSFUL EGGS, AS LARGER ONES MAY DISTORT THE SHAPE AS THEY OPEN.

# EASTER
# FEASTS

Following Lent, Easter is a time of feasting. Time to enjoy scrumptious egg breakfasts, decoratively laid out on seasonal tables, countless afternoon snacks and main meals of delicious juicy meats delicately flavored with spring herbs and accompanied by tender young vegetables.

# MAD HATTER'S TEA PARTY

## SANDWICH PLATTER
*Makes 64 triangles*

*20 slices brown bread*
*1 stick butter, softened*
*2 cucumbers, thinly sliced*
*12 slices white bread*
*crisp green salad leaves, such as*
*watercress, rocket, or lettuce*

### SALMON FILLING
*14¾ oz. can red salmon*
*1 tbs. powdered gelatine*
*1 cup mayonnaise or*
*heavy cream*
*1 tbs. lemon juice*
*1 tbs. ketchup*
*pepper*

### EGG AND ANCHOVY FILLING
*8 canned anchovy fillets, well drained*
*4 tbs. mayonnaise*
*6 hard-boiled eggs, shelled*
*pepper*

To make the salmon filling, drain and reserve juice from the salmon but discard any skin and bones. Dissolve the gelatin in 3 tbs. cold water in a small saucepan over very gentle heat.

Place the mayonnaise or cream, lemon juice, and ketchup in a food processor and whizz in the gelatin. Add the salmon with its liquid and pulse quickly to combine but keep a slightly rough texture. Season to taste with pepper.

Transfer to a dish, cover with plastic wrap, and chill for at least 3 hours until firmly set. (This can be made up to 48 hours in advance and kept, covered, in the refrigerator.)

To make the egg and anchovy filling, mash the anchovy fillets to a paste on a plate or board with the back of a round-ended knife. Combine well with the mayonnaise. Mash the eggs and stir into the anchovy-flavored mayonnaise. Season generously with pepper.

To make the sandwiches, spread a generous amount of salmon filling on 10 slices of lightly buttered brown bread and top with thinly sliced cucumber. Season to taste. Top each with a second slice of lightly buttered bread and remove the crusts. Cut the sandwiches into 40 triangles.

Spread a generous amount of egg and anchovy filling on 6 slices of lightly buttered white bread and top with crisp green salad leaves. Top each with a second slice of lightly buttered bread. Remove the crusts and cut the sandwiches into 24 triangles. Cover with plastic wrap if not serving at once.

*RIGHT* A DELICIOUS SPREAD OF DAINTY
SANDWICHES, EASTER BONNET COOKIES,
AND CHOCOLATE GATEAU.

## CONTRIBUTORS

Karin Cafazzo-Hossack (batik eggs pp.28-31, springtime sweater pp.60-5)
32 Petley Road, London W6 9ST
(071 386 9748)

Carluccio's (pasta nests pp. 44-5)
30 Neal Street, London WC2H 9PS
(071 240 1487)

Shane Connolly (fresh flowers pp.76-89)
7 Bracewell Road, London W10 6AE
(081 964 4398)

Georgina Crowder (gilded eggs pp. 32-3)
(081 673 3641) or at Abbey Frames
(071 622 4815)

Jamboree (appliqué children's clothes pp.66-7)
c/o Barnshill Cottage, Thornden Lane,
Rolvenden Layne, Rolvenden,
Nr Cranbrook, Kent

Alison Jenkins (Easter bonnets pp.68-71)
36 Crystal Palace Road, London SE22 9HB

Susan Moxley (papier-mâché gift boxes pp. 46-9)
33 Edith Road, Grandpont,
Oxford OX1 4QB (0865 251396)

Jane Packer (topiary eggs pp. 94-7)
56 James Street, London W1M 5HS
(071 935 2673)

Juliette Pearce (papier-mâché egg cup pp.58-9)
Cross Street Studios, 14 Cross Street,
Hove BN3 1AJ (0273 725321)

Martin Robinson (egg and feather wreath pp.50-1, spring urns pp.74-5, moss rabbit pp.90-1)
Martin Robinson Flowers, Thomas Neal's,
Earlham Street, London WC2H 9LD
(071 379 3201)

Royal School of Needlework (cross-stitch sampler pp.52-3)
Apartment 12a, Hampton Court Palace, East Molesey, Surrey KT8 9AU
(081 943 1432)

Deborah Schneebeli-Morrell (natural dyed eggs pp. 24-5, engraved eggs pp. 26-7, papercut cards pp.54-7)
10 York Rise, London NW5 1SS

Mark at Juliet Willis (dried flower nest pp. 92-3)
336 Old York Road, London SW18 1SS
(081 874 9944)

Basia Zarzycka (beaded eggs pp. 34-7)
135 King's Road, London SW3 4PW
(071 351 7276)

## SUPPLIERS

ART/CRAFT/GRAPHIC
Charrette
212 East 54th Street
New York, NY 10022

Eaglecrafts, Inc.
168 W. 12th Street
Ogden, UT 84404
(801) 393-3991

New York Central
62 Third Avenue
New York, NY 10003
(212) 473-7705

Sam Flax
425 Park Avenue
New York, NY 10022
(212) 620-3060

PAINT
Janovic Plaza
161 Sixth Avenue
New York, NY 10014
(212) 627-1100

Pearl Paint Company
308 Canal Street
New York, NY 10013
(212) 431-7932

JEWELRY/BEADS/ORNAMENTS
Ornamental Resources
P.O. Box 3013
Idaho Springs, CO 80542
(303) 279-2102

SEWING/KNITTING
Erica Wilson Needle Works
717 Madison Avenue
New York, NY 10021
(212) 832-7290

Halcyon Yarns
12 School Street
Bath, ME 04530
(207) 442-7909

# INDEX